"The experience of Warning Light Calling returns me to a sense of dis-place, it's Europe, but parallel. Distended into Sputnik's imaginative and creatively frustrated world. A sense of beneficial strangeness and emotional normalcy abounds in Warning Light Calling. The desperate and sometimes beset mind of Sputnik. Yelena's commanding but supportive if sometimes distant stare. Threaded through is the frustration of the last two years, of disconnection within the realm of fictional Aarhus, and paused breath of the planet. A tripped out, cathartic and desperate ride through dissidence, flower guns and space stations, which if we're not careful, will eat us alive."

Sapha Burnell, Author of Usurper Kings, Son of Abel & Neon Lieben

"Westergard's excellent poetry collection depicts "hygge" in its various aspects as practiced or rendered in the outskirts of Denmark....Westergard is definitely a talent to look for in the future!"

The Praire Book Review

"This small volume could work well in any language. The varied themes and images reach out and embrace the reader.

In Peter Graarup Westergaard's Danish Northwest/Hygge Poems from the Outskirts, the reader is drawn into the forms and themes as easily as reading a folktale."

North of Oxford Press

"The people and places described in Danish Northwest are complicated but distinct. As you read this collection you will be a guest in their lives, a visitor to their world. Faced with the great unknown of the future, you'll likely find yourself wondering fervently what might come next for them.

Overall, reading Peter Graarup Westergaard's work has a soothing and calming effect on your soul. Culturally informative and entertaining, Danish Northwest is a delightful read. Take a break from your hectic lifestyle and spend some time in Thy, absorbing these hygge poems from the outskirts."

Indies Today

"The joy for the little things of the world around us is incessantly reverberated in this poetic journey. Overall, the collection presents a lively atmosphere to the reader providing an interactive gathering of 'Hygge' practice. With all its simplicity and purity, this collection propels the reader to newer and greener lands populated with solace and peace."

Muse India

WARNING LIGHT CALLING

PETER GRAARUPWESTERGAARD

VRÆYDA
LITERARY

Vræyda Literary
An Imprint of
Vræyda Multimedia Inc, Port Coquitlam
www.vraeydamedia.ca | petergraarupwestergaard.com

Editing by Lis Goryniuk-Ratajczak
Cover by Marissa Wagner
Cover Photography by Unsplash

Printed in the UK

First Printing, 2016 10 9 8 7 6 5 4 3 2
ISBN: 978-1-988034-17-1 (Paperback)
ISBN: 978-1-988034-18-8 (eBook)

Vræyda Literary brings authors to your event. For information, to bulk purchase or book an event contact ambassador@vraeydamedia.ca.

TOC

Foreword

by Lis Goryniuk-Ratajczak

When *Warning Light Calling* came across my desk, the first poem I read was 'Dear Spacey Peter', "forced into a work placement, BECAUSE I have been in outer space for so long". Poetry bathed in cyberpunk day dreams and Homeric love triangles gripped my attention, and I remember looking up from the computer only when the last stanza "laid the poems down in a golden shrine" (Space. Disappearance. Zero). Peter Graarup Westergaard delivered more than wild iconoclasm against a fictional monocultural state, within the frame of a fictional Denmark. Doused in the style of Soviet Dissident poets, layers of allusions to Homer's Trojan lovers, Warning Light Calling wrapped in the tin-foil tactics of a space marine, who attempted to bite back from "Comrade Corona"'s isolation. Working with Peter was a joy and a brief deepening of connection to Scandinavian roots.

Protagonist Sputnik is one part iconoclast and one part madness. A dissident poet steeped in the battle against monoculture and the disease of disquiet. One pass gave a firm allusion to Homer, the next Dostoevsky. As heteroglossic as Mikhail Bakhtin, filled with distinct layers of conceptualized world views within the same poems. Language in *Warning Light Calling* is mutable through cultural exchange. Like Bakhtin's 'Discourse in the Novel', *Warning Light Calling* attempted to combat the tension between centralized and decentralized order. To echo both the call to sit down and chill out during the early days of the Pandemic, and the frustration of post-soviet dissidence roaring for freedom from the machine.

At once all of the above, *Warning Light Calling* is pandemic narrative, fractured love story, dissident imprisonment, space odyssey and current Scandinavian life-ballad. While that multiplicity can at some points be difficult to grasp without a moment of priming, *Warning Light Calling* is worth the effort. It is sublimation: both gas and solid; it dives through the visceral weight of political constraint, while ending beyond the clouds into a space station from whence Sputnik required escape. It is ephemeral, yet grounded in a fractured image, through the unreliable narration of Sputnik (Spacey Peter) and his many break-downs. Sputnik's fictional biography comes next, via Peter Graarup Westergaard. The triumph of being the off-console Chosen One is sloughed off the moment he grasps hold of the controller, and becomes another fallen image, another man whose on-and-off Yelena (think Helene of Troy) foreshadows the final off.

Clever, responsive, dissociative and deep into gamer culture, Warning Light Calling is the gamer grown-up. A cultural entity, whose adolescent desire to win in-game is marred by the responsibilities of a life restrained.

Warning Light Calling is best read in the lens of Homeric epics dressed in new clothes. The outfit is a space suit, with Cosmonaut bleached off and a faint horse's head clad in a surgical mask its replacement. The sort of poetry which convicts, unsettles, briefly mollifies, then leaves the reader within dangerous and dissident minds. Is the world such a different place than in history? How does a gamer-guy like Sputnik handle being both chosen one and relegated second-string to Don Paris in Yelena's eyes? "And yet I trespass everything to the boundaries. Use rules, God, and the dialectics of Marx, Soviet law and the traffic laws of the universe, and I bend them as I please" (The Great Escape). Once viewed as a form of anger against the "large airless vacuum" of repressive pandemic society, it becomes a recycled breath, begging for fresh air. *Warning Light Calling* reminds of both scream and nuanced argument painted in duo-chromatics with a fishbowl helmet left off for size.

Warning Light Calling was made for the off-kilter poetry absorber. Anyone who wanted to dig into the ancient, with their head so far in the clouds it's reached past the stratosphere and around the moon. As a work of poetry, it's a variable and gripping collection of beats. Sometimes metal, sometimes House. Off-kilter in a way Homer never was, *Warning Light Calling* takes the mythic triad of Helene, Menelaus and Paris and un-grounds it into the dissident tale of Yelena, Sputnik and Don Paris "means nothing to me. 'Really?' Don't you want to leave him a message?" (Oh Denmark's Radio). Surrounding the Trojan triangle is the frustrated impetus of Sputnik for a world without the restraints of COVID-19, of space stations like Gulags and chosen ones firmly within the body pneumatic.

Wild, contained by the press of contagion in this fictional Denmark, *Warning Light Calling* is both ode, nodal origin point of spacey new waves and the listless attempt of a man to find his space. Please enjoy the (fictional) introduction to Spacey Peter, our 'hero' Sputnik, written by Peter on the next page. And further on, to Sputnik's *Warning Light Calling*.

Sputnik Peter - the Cosmonaut 8000

Sputnik: Russian for "companion"
or "spouse"—is also a name applied
to certain spacecraft launched
under the Soviet space program.
—Russiapedia

1

Who was Sputnik? I made a considerable amount of research into Sputnik's life beyond the time I knew him, limited to a few years. I know he lived in Aarhus from 2012 to 2021, and during that period, he earned an MA in the History of Ideas, with a minor in Russian literature. He finished his thesis in 2017 in a standard amount of time. So he lived up to the Danish government's goals for quick progress in studies, and in many ways, was a role model student. Besides that, there was nothing of the conformer about him. Sputnik wrote his master's thesis on Soviet futuristic ideas, especially concerning future utopias or dystopias. I know Sputnik was writing or planning on writing a collection of essays based on his studies in Soviet futuristic thought. The present book is entirely devoted to his speculative futuristic poetry—maybe fragments of this poetry—from the manuscript *WARNING LIGHT CALLING* which he sent to me before his disappearance, and which can be seen as his late tribute to red thinking in a spacey sci-fi version. *WARNING LIGHT CALLING* was written or completed during the Covid-19 pandemic—that shows clearly in the imagery and narration—the manuscript is also a kind of "witness literature".

After graduation and a period of a few months' unemployment, Sputnik began to work within a new psychiatry project in 2018. This project was largely based on the insights from newly invented psychiatric approaches and hardly tested neuroscience. He also started working as a supervisor through a psychotherapist training program and participated in a number of experiments at the psychiatric hospital in Aarhus, until it closed due to several serious scandals, extensively covered in the media. Sputnik was, of course, also affected by these scandals. Although he worked only on the periphery, he was able to observe what was going on around him. It cannot be ruled out these experiences helped shape his deep dissident criticism and drew him toward a fundamental critique you find in all his poetry.

Sputnik was also hit by a creative vein of madness. This is especially seen in his literary sci-fi texts, some of which are reproduced here. But it is seen in his essays, which, unfortunately, have not yet been published in aggregated form. I do not know if he went into therapy, beyond the therapy he was given for the training as a supervisor. At least a profound knowledge of the strange manifestations of the human mind is clear in the poems—which suggests he had a strap of the skin himself.

2

Sputnik's birth name was Peter Larsen Hardt, and he was born in Hanstholm in Thy in 1993. He grew up as the oldest of four siblings in a harmonious family, where both his father and mother worked in the fishing industry in Hanstholm. His father was born in Thy, but his mother was originally from Canada, and this, partly, explains his English-language inclinations. His parents met when his father was working on a farm outside Vancouver as a volunteer.

Sputnik graduated from Thisted Gymnasium at eighteen years old, which was quite young, according to Danish standards. During his time in high school, he formed a socialist avant-garde e-sport team called *The Sputniks*. He was a competent punk gamer and primarily played the end game leader. There are many stories about this team, one of which is they were good at gaming but bad at wooing women.

I met Sputnik one day at a writing seminar at *Poetklub Aarhus* on the Soviet writer Mikhail Bulgakov. Sputnik was young; his red hair shoulder-length, and green-grey eyes looked out over the conference room while one of the established writers lectured with a monotonous, Burroughs-like intonation. Exactly what Sputnik looked for, I don't know. Perhaps girls, maybe boys, perhaps faraway golden satellites, or an unknown meteor's dangerous path into his star-studded sky? At any rate, the girls discovered him; they gathered around without him paying any attention at all.

Surely, Sputnik had a huge "attitude problem", especially in regard to authorities and institutions. If someone required something, he responded by doing the exact opposite. He had a distinct role as a dissident right from his youth. And as one can guess, Sputnik could be rude, and I frequently told him so. But he wasn't a coward. Even though he was rather inflated, there was always something that affixed to reality, albeit with a strong provoking sarcastic approach.

He quit his job in the psychiatric system, and settled as a hot-dog vendor at Store Torv in Aarhus. This might have been his biggest job success, although he could not keep the commitment going in the long run. In fact, he only worked in the hot-dog business for two summers and left, with no further reason. It is unclear to me what he earned his money from. To the best of my knowledge, he did not receive unemployment benefits or social assistance. Yet it was precisely in his "hot-dog period" he developed his socialist sci-fi poetry, which meant many people came to the hot-dog stand and had a hot dog and a vision of the future.

3

Sputnik wrote hardline futuristic and speculative sci-fi poetry as an expression of his intense dissident criticism. The poems are written in the tradition of slam, beat and punk poetry, with striking expressions that reveal his past as a gamer. The outsider theme is present everywhere—Sputnik is at once sick, crazy, and unemployed. Social indignation is a central feeling of all his poems. But Sputnik is neither mentally ill nor mentally healthy; he is in a position outside the normal distinctions, in a place where speculative sci-fi poetry is created.

Variability and fast movement characterize Sputnik's poetry, and his writing is a poetic response to the organized, fixed, and dogmatic nature of our society. Sputnik never goes straight to poetry but chooses the inaccurate, offbeat, and almost impassable way into the future. To Sputnik, the artist is an outsider who is excluded from the community, the world and the present reality. Sometimes he speaks as Sputnik in the first person; sometimes about Sputnik in the third, almost as an omniscient narrator; and sometimes it is hard to detect a fixed narrator at all. Sometimes he writes fiction, yet sometimes it is also non-fiction, one never knows. But his poetry is always futuristic and visionary, almost prophetic.

The allusions to the ancient epics, the *Iliad* and the *Odyssey*, are not without cause. In his poetry, he seems to imagine the future of Aarhus as his Troy. He believes himself to be one of the noble defenders of Aarhus in the future; he is an uncompromising space warrior against any conformity and claims of equality. He is both a hero and an anti-hero, and in his own eyes, he is a unique individual who was placed here on the earth to fight normality and normative thinking.

WARNING LIGHT CALLING is intentionally structured as the war against Troy as described in the *Iliad*, and the journey into space is modelled after parts of the *Odyssey*, both with significant deviations from the ancient epics. But the main course follows some of the episodes in the *Iliad* and the *Odyssey*, only with the important change that the setting is a strange futuristic Aarhus—yet imagined from Sputnik's personal (anti-)Soviet space. The characters resemble real people, but they also gained traits from their mythological Greek and Soviet ancestors. *WARNING LIGHT CALLING* depicts several characters from a Soviet context, and in a sense, they resemble the Achaeans in the *Iliad* who attack the people of Troy. They attacked Aarhus (Troy) because they want to take control of the city, infuse the future citizens of Aarhus with a "new consciousness," and change the consciousness of our protagonist, Sputnik.

As a consequence, significant parts of *WARNING LIGHT CALLING* consist of tributes to dissident Soviet authors and thinkers—Osip Mandelstam, Vladimir Mayakovsky, Alexander Belyaev, Mikhail Bulgakov, Alexey N. Tolstoy, Mikhail Bakhtin, Isaac Babel, Boris Pasternak, Andrei Tarkovsky, Isaiah Berlin, Vladimir Nabokov and Joseph Brodsky. Not all of them are sci-fi writers or thinkers, but Sputnik was greatly influenced. Above all the writers, Fyodor Dostoevsky has a special significance in Sputnik's narrative poems; he seems to resemble the character Tiresias as a seer and a mystic. To some degree they were all fellow dissidents, and Sputnik felt they were on his side in his fight against authorities and institutions of all kinds.

Sputnik used the Soviet liberal dissidents in his imaginary and futuristic fight against what he called "Team Red Army". I often heard him speak of Team Red

Army, and of course, he meant this metaphorically and ironically. Sometimes it even sounded like he was the end team leader of this brigade. In some sense, one could understand the character 'Sputnik Peter' as a futuristic version of the Soviet tale "Peter the Wolf". In the *WARNING LIGHT CALLING,* Sputnik generally applied these conceptions from dissident Soviet culture and literature to create a vision of a near-futuristic Aarhus which also is an interpretation of societal illnesses in his own contemporary time and life.

Sputnik believed in poetry as a kind of self-therapy, as unfolded in the strong erotic element in many of Sputnik's poems, which was partly inspired by his somewhat ambiguous relationship with his muse and on-off girlfriend, Yelena. However, a close reading of *WARNING LIGHT CALLING* will reveal a major part of the collection deals with the troublesome relationship with Yelena as it turns into a "ménage à trois" between Sputnik, Yelena, and Don Paris. This love triangle might be the real offspring of Sputnik's dissidence and the reason for his later disappearance. I've tried to find Yelena and Don Paris, but have proven unsuccessful in both instances. Nobody knows who they are. Maybe they were invented by his imagination?

In the beginning, I thought I was the model for some of the characters in *WARNING LIGHT CALLING.* Sputnik always bullied me because of my lack of interest in the transgressive and futuristic. To his disappointment, there were no dissident character traits in me. He wanted me to transgress myself, participate in semi-dissident activities, and so on. But I avoided such luring from his side. I can easily see how these poems could also be a parodic replication of who I am not and what he wished me to be. Yet I am not sure if I am the only source of inspiration for his characters. Some of the patients he met via his work at the psychiatric hospital might also have given him ideas. One young man had a huge influence on Sputnik at a certain period. He came to stand as the model hero for him, a bit how Deleuze and Guattari described the schizophrenic hero in *L'anti-Œdipe. Capitalisme et schizophrénie.* Who knows, maybe he is the real Sputnik of the poems?

English was Sputnik's choice of language because he wanted to communicate his visions internationally. He had some megalomaniac tendencies, to say the least. But there was also some reason for it; his mother is from the Vancouver area (but descended from Russian immigrants). The English language was his mother tongue, whereas his father tongue would have been "Thybomål," and in this respect, he felt freer to express himself without any restraints in the English language rather than in Danish. Writing in Danish did not appeal. He grew up speaking the Danish dialect, Thybomål, which, in a sense, is not really standard Danish but rather another language with its own grammatical rules, in some instances similar to English. He learned English extensively in the Danish school system since he was eight or nine, and while attending university, wrote all his assignments in English. Additionally, he lived in Vancouver, trying to break through as a professional gamer while working on a fishing fleet in his sabbatical year after high school. Some would say he mastered written English better than written Danish.

4

Sputnik was "the exemplary hot-dog vendor on the moon", as one of his professors at university joked. However, he is now also one of the missing persons whom the famous Danish television program *Som sunket i jorden* stopped trying to find. From the program, it appeared Sputnik had apparently been in the northernmost part of Canada. Since then, no one has seen him, and no one knows if he is dead or alive. The Covid-pandemic has not made it easier to find him.

Before leaving on his journey in the middle of the Covid-19-pandemic, Sputnik Peter sent the following manuscript to me, which I now publish because these poems or prose pieces should be known to a wider public. This manuscript is also the last communication I had from him. At the time of writing this, ten months passed since he disappeared. I have edited the manuscript only a little, and corrected a few obvious grammatical errors or typos, although I also, in several places, indirectly appear in Sputnik's manuscript. *WARNING LIGHT CALLING* is based Peter Larsen Hardt's life in the years before the pandemic and his experiences of the pandemic in the first months. However, this book is truly his warning light calling of "being Sputnik" in the future of Aarhus, Denmark.

—Mr. W.P.
The only begetter of these ensuing poems.

Prelude

*During the morning I improved my sense of orientation
in the city by taking a long walk along the inner boulevards.*

~ Walter Benjamin.

Space. Sample. Love

I will tell the world about the demon who grabbed me
and who raged in anguish the thousands of planets.
Whole multitudes of young comrades were obsessed and infected,
and made prey to space soldiers and strange, unidentified birds—
I will tell the earth about that moment when poetry and love
made me go Sputnik.

Club Moscow in Aarhus

Yelena grabbed my harness,
I was afraid of her. She was
a woman of the night;
between the black iron
mountains, she had a glare
like sunflowers from
a forbidden spring.

I left my home space moon
for a parachute stretched
over the earthly sphere
like a huge pink canopy bed.

Oh Denmark's Radio

"Now we've been talking
all morning." Drill stick
and German techno—Neither of us
with the required edge
for scoring at Club Moscow.

I've never been focused.
"I know that so well."
Don Paris means
nothing to me. "Really?"
Don't you want to leave him
a message? "Spacey Peter,
all I need is Denmark's
Gosteleradio."

I'm concerned about your
inner radio. "You believe in
redness." Let's change beds."
And play the Soviet troika
again."

Danish Dream

Come on. I'm also a liberal John
who likes to have sex in the forest.
On the little mattress in the inner room
when it's a freaking hot summer
and the steaks are on the grill
soaked with American marinade
in the US suburbs
where we can live a quiet life
with no existential themes
and a garbage can full of dirty condoms.
But, holy shit, Yelena
doesn't like I am reading
William S. Burroughs's dirty novels
because he was a crazy fuck,
and because she is afraid
I might be a crazy fuck as well.
"But come on," I say to her.
"I am no William Tell."
I'm the liberal John of your forest.

I can go deep into the woods.
Only wearing my lumberjack shirt,
I can shoot cuckoos in the clouds.

Rainbow Forest

How hot we were the other day
lying in another bunker, getting
a Blooming Wizard and an Aura Flora.
We were fit as poodles in a new forest
fell in the pond and could not help
sniffing out the deep peat moss
as nature's greatest happiness-dogs.
We walked the rainbow in the sky,
made a wealthy crane city
out of our fleshy spines. Every naked
flower yearned to go upstairs with us
where the mirage of the universe
could be seen with every color reflected
by a distant neon machine in the clouds
of golden rain and utopian sun.

Peace in Our Time

Yelena rushes up
                to her castle   on the hill.
She is looking for
                a new bird.

Her budgie flew   out of its cage.
                              "—My Sputnik."

Now the Danish   satellite   is famous

      for providing   the best offspring.

"—Who says?"
                I think she's so masculine.

"—Smartphones will kiss me.
                Of pure jealousy.

Obviously, I think she has a   hot body."

Shall we dance?
         "—It is completely   unforgivable

to ask me about that   right now."

So which one of us actually

                                    got it wrong?

My words have become hers,

                and I will do everything   she says.

I'm the alarm clock   who has always   called her

across countless numbers   of reincarnations.

TOO SWEET.

Once upon a time, we were
the Master and Margarita,
or Lara and Zhivago, or even
Vronsky and Anna Karenina.

But Yelena has to travel
                    away from me
and stay out
                    on the vast moonland
                                    of pure shamans.

Canned Ham

my on-off girlfriend yel
ena the author of the inf
amous pamphlet the uns
toppable ham argued for
liberating sexuality from
ham production and intr
oduce a tough ham polic
y yelena had been afraid
of the hams since she not
iced her own belly being
invaded she was convinc
ed the ham could devour
her totally she kept a wat
chful eye on the wobblin
g ham, who had occupie
d first her body then the
playpen in her living roo
m yelena knew from her
book, l'anti-oedipe the h
am would grow into a vi
brating meat mass the ha
m had begun to grow tee
th (it was all don paris' f
ault) yelena had to sell th
e little meatball to a skill
ed cannery it was import
ant to get rid of it as lon
g as it was still harmless

Space Jealousy

My dearest Yelena, I hovered
in space with black stars
whenever you messaged me.

I watched you for hours converse
with the beautiful Don Paris,
he answered with laughter.

I hid behind the skies,
watching him kiss you,
his hands at your breast.

Despite my bad conscience,
I floated noiselessly in the air.
A black hole absorbed my bones.

Comrades. Distance. Unemployed.

Red Space Warriors like us, with strength and wisdom,
will lead by brave example.
We will battle the citizens of Aarhus and reveal a new ideology.
We are the unwary comrades who will provoke
by the works of climate changes and university knowledge.

Shoot Out

After the space race:
most intricate flowers
SHOOT OUT, later
the sky takes it hard.
All you get is one
lazy flower gun,
the survival of the earth
is not at all possible.
Your whole life
breaks into diamonds.
I am the chilly one
of incredible things,
yet it's hard to continue
when you get space sickness.
You get sores all over.

Funniest Game Ever

Fifty-two Danish villains
attacked the slaughterhouse,
two of the crooks were called
"the joke sausages."
They had a secret aromatic
machine making rubber teeth.
As it was spacey red
it could be sold for more
than one million rubles
next to the plastic boxes.
Yet eight heroes pulled out,
but "the joke sausages"
smoked a chill feature.

Heaven Big File

I lay in the backyard of a moon space,
without having any package sent over.
Heaven was a big file;
A gigantic flash went farther than the sun.
It was as good as a real supernova laser.
Yet, I had to get it out of orbit
to keep the wave steady
in the evening for a couple of hours.

Wall On Orbit

In the same Siberian Western,
I slid into space - I am
represented completely,
melted into one thing
while I shout: "My identity
is unlimited, distributed."

Yippie ki-yay, I am
a space cowboy. I travel
freely and interwoven
in the global twist
with full compensation
for the bad taste
on national fried mink day.

Hi, ho, I am a hero.
You are nobody.
There is no I
in front of the wall
to my mental prairie.

Dear Spacey Peter

I'm forced

        into a work placement,

BECAUSE

          I have been in outer space for so long.

But I've taken my precautions,

    I know very well

        of their new procedures.

They send unemployed

        dissidents,
        philosophers
        and poets

to work at the old factories,

        to work as newspaper boys,

and what do I know?

Has bourgeois Denmark

        embarked on a new

          labor-camp policy,

where they make dissidents

                work with their invisible hands?

"YOU CAN JUST AS WELL FEED PIGS WITH DISSIDENTS"

        they yell on Denmark's Radio.

One of these days

           I will invite my dissident comrades

to my ballroom apartment in   8000 Aarhus C,

             and we'll burn our

writings

in the middle of the floor,

        sing hallelujah,

            drink, and

                watch football.

Climate. Plague. Testing.

"Prophet of plagues, forever testing!"
Still must my tongue some wounding message bring.
And still my red pride provoke the city of Aarhus,
alas, for this falsehood is my true prophesy.

Shake Hands, Climate

Close your eyes,

         people   live suspiciously

in squeaky houses   with isolated odors

and refuse to talk

              to each other about it.

It does not look good, folks.

Push the sunglasses   back down.

The dangerous   *disintegration syndrome*

infects everyone   by touch.

The remains are extremely   infectious.

A body part is suddenly   disintegrated

and turns into a lump of puffy grease

in   the middle of   the clean linoleum floor.

One day,   the old city   will be flooded

with soapy water,
washed out of the hot world map.
1 iped out with a rag of a gigantic wave,
and all the so-called

legitimate citizens

will have

left.

Yet No Contamination

The first to become ill are the traveling merchants, the troubadours, the clerics, and the scholars. They have all been infected elsewhere and bring the plague to like-minded kin; then the secular powers-that-be become ill because they have close contact with travelers of different kinds, not least when seeking advice and guidance. Thus, as people of power compress to crumble and drudge off to their big homes, they are infected with the plague. At home, they get sick and die without help. The rats, which have always run ahead, spread the plague from below, from the sewers, making the plague spread even further, passing it on to small merchants and craftsmen. Finally, the plague hits the surrounding farms, and at the end: the hunter who has been in the forest for many days.

Alas, during this black death I am in outer space, completely uncontaminated and alone.

The Health-Care System

Dr.
Plato Sam
Garin completely
eradicated all diseases
with his vaccine. Hurray!
No pandemic diseases existed
anymore: Chikungunya, Cholera,
Crimean-Congo hemorrhagic fever,
Ebola virus disease, Hendra virus infection,
Influenza, Lassa fever, Marburg virus disease,
Meningitis, MERS-CoV, Monkeypox, Nipah virus
infection, Coronavirus, Plague, Rift Valley fever, SARS,
Smallpox, Tularaemia, Yellow fever, Zika virus disease, as well as
HIV, AIDS, Syphilis and Gonorrhoea were extinguished like negligible
species from the rainforests. *Ura! Ura!* Of course, the natural selection of the
rainforest, in a counterattack, dragged the human species to the biodynamic gallows,
muahaha. Now the worst human infection would be finally crucified: the wicked language.

Oops.

It Feels Like

Comrade Corona

        has sent me

                in isolation.

He has

        deprived me of

                my freedom.

With a cotton swab

        my space helmet

                is crushed apart,

stabbed

        as a trowel

                into my internal soft mechanics.

        I cannot say a word.

I swallow

        my brain in

                the humanitarian show trials:

"TESTING IS MY CONSCIOUSNESS."

The state has to

                protect itself

                                against its citizens.

I belong to

                the system,

            among the secret files

                              of experiment.

Jab, jab, the body papers are stamped,

              vaccine passports

                          are the only legitimate

access to

the open-

closed post-pandemic society.

Machine. Tales. Ideas.

They are hiding, concealed in a metal contraption;
they have built a machine to use against the walls,
to spy on the homes, or fall on the city from above,
or it hides some other trick: People of Aarhus,
don't trust this machine.

The Trojan Love Machine

I knew this girl who was a storyteller. I will call her Diotima. She had nut-dark brown eyes and a dark complexion. Her slightly distant gaze suggested a large inner world.

We strolled through the streets of our city every evening, and one day, she decided to tell me the story about The Trojan Love Machine. I was thrilled, because I was a great fan of love-stories, although not an experienced practitioner of love myself, to say the least.

*

I had to imagine The Trojan Love Machine as a large contraption standing on the main square in a famous city, she told me. This machine could think both in circles and in boxes, and gradually, it came to grow by itself; flowers shot up its back; it multiplied in thick reddish or greenish meaty plates on all sides, they arranged themselves in layers like wooden rings or meat fibers, and the machine became more and more alive.

At the front end of the machine, an exit gradually formed, where one could imagine this monster horse would spit out truths about love. And at the back end, a small hole was visible, which eventually became a hatch nobody yet knew what use it might have. And it hummed immensely, Diotima told me.

*

The machine was the newest invention of a loveless people who were living in a famous city, not so far from here, Diotima explained. Any kind of natural love-making was forbidden in this famous city for many years, due to a plague and it was instated by law that no one was allowed to practice or even think about love. I meant, of course, the loveless people occasionally felt frustrated, and also felt a certain meaninglessness and alienation towards each other. The practice of making love was now forgotten, and many young people never heard of it, though they might have a feeling of something trembling from time to time.

The people of the city divided into two opposing groups: men and women, who were not allowed to interfere, nor wished to either. But now this humming machine stood in the middle of the square and seemed tempting. Maybe it wanted something to tell the people of the famous city?

Diotima stopped for a while and looked at me. I know she was looking for an excuse to keep on telling me the story while we walked the streets this night.

*

It all started, she continued, when an old woman from the old part of the city revealed that she knew the secret about love from her youth many years ago.

One day, without anyone seeing it, she told this secret to a young man from the neighbourhood. But he went out into the streets of the city where he proclaimed the message he had received from the old woman. Every single place he went, he said: "The truth of love is always to be found with the man and masculinity. Ask a man and you will know the nature of love."

Yet the next day, a woman who came to him said she heard somewhere else, from a man who believed he knew the nature of love, that the truth of love is always to be found with the woman and femininity.

Now, suddenly, the loveless people woke from their loveless dream. They knew something was missing. It was in these moments, the people of the city turned to the God of love, and said to him: "Please, God come and help us in these difficult and tormenting times. Tell us the true nature of love." He listened to their outcry from the ceiling of a church, but decided not to intervene.

*

Since the people of the city received no answer, they decided to build a love machine that could tell them the truth about love. But it was not easy, because the women and the men could not agree on building the machine jointly, so they built parts separately and later combined them. The machine came to stand in the middle of the square of a famous city between the women's group and the men's group, right in the middle.

The calculation method of the machine would consist of only two elements, namely, a male component and a female component, which in turn could be stretched to an infinite number of combinations. In this way, the machine would be able to devise the truth about love for both sides of the city.

There was a buzzing and humming about the machine, it resembled something that had to throw up everything it contained. It also began to smell bad like vomit, as it rumbled out gases. Suddenly it gave up and freed itself from everything it had in its interior. There was a stench around it of unknown dirty secretions, and it was not easy to see anything in the cloud of truth-tinkering, Diotima assured me.

*

Yet the people were amazed by this growing beast, maybe it could be the answer to all their unfulfilled dreams. But first they wanted to make it speak, and to explain their situation and move the people of the city to unbelievable levels of consciousness. Maybe the humming machine on the middle of the square could be their saviour and tell the truth about love?

Finally, the machine began to speak:
"A man and a woman have to lie inside me," it said.
The people were pale with fear to learn that a man and a woman would have to lie together.

In the beginning, they rejected the straight order from the machine. But the machine insisted with its whole massiveness. The two groups talked together to find a suitable couple to climb into the back of the machine. There were not many who wanted to lie down in the smelly beast, and not at all with one from the other gender.

*

But the people of the city nevertheless found a young couple. She came from the sweet valley, and he from a mountain plateau far away. The people thought the two of them could easily be lured to lie inside the machine.

They were so naïve and gullible, and so it was said, made eyes at each other. Of course, the two young people declined initially, but all the citizens of the city encouraged, "Well, come on, do it for our sake—come on now." And finally, they agreed to open the hatch and crawl into the back of the humming machine. Time passed—maybe a whole hour went by—and the two young people came out again.

And what sight the two crowds experienced. The young couple were totally absorbed in one another, which was against all rules and all morals of the city, and they were completely inseparable. They kissed from top to bottom—and touched each other where it was not legal.

It was abominable for the rival groups to look at; a man and a woman should stay completely apart. But as time went on, the citizens of the city could see the two were happy with each other, and it didn't take long before there was another couple, this time not quite young anymore, who wanted to try the machine, although they, of course, hated each other to the core, the couple assured all the people of the city.

This couple also came out of the machine changed, and infatuated, so the people of the city called for law and order. However, the people also wanted to learn. What happened in there? And soon there was a new couple ready to climb into the machine, and before long, a queue began to form behind the contraption.

Now all the inhabitants of the city wanted to try a trip inside the big beast. Men and men, women and women, everybody in all kinds of combinations wanted a ride in the box. "Yes, yes; come hither," The Trojan Love Machine said, and the people stood in line while waiting for bliss.

*

From his holy ceiling, the God of love followed the festivities and thought the people of the city were now too much. For a moment, he went down to the earth among the people in the queue.

"Stop this. Go home to yourselves."

And he gave the machine a proper kick in the ass, so it fell apart. It sounded like the puncturing of dough. The machine went puff, and all the pleasures on the square stopped. The bliss disappeared, but the people of the city felt strangely relieved and again discovered the true nature of love, Diotima told me.

PETER GRAARUP WESTERGAARD

I looked at Diotima, and she looked at me. By a strange coincidence, we were now standing on the main square of our city. And as it happened, a circus arrived to the city, and we saw a gigantic strange box, with plants and vegetation growing on all sides of it. This magic box was installed in the middle of the great square. People were already standing in queue for the fun to happen. We looked at it, and without any hesitation, we walked straight away from the ticket booth, as if we knew what to expect.

The Museum of Ideas

Only barbarians are not curious
about where they come from, how
they came to be where they are,
where they appear to be going,
whether they wish to go there, and
if so, why, and if not, why not.
—*Isaiah Berlin*

From the corner of a comfortable
what-I-am-not, I woke up from
my reality-dream and found myself
working at the Museum of Ideas
as a common custodian who shows foreigners
the exhibition on everyday thoughts
when they ask what they really are.

A name tag on my left tells me who I am.
Yet the exhibition to the right makes me
alienated. My shirt is green-blue-red,
a signal of the general identity question.
Nothing is meant for the caged hens of ontology.
"No joking in here, please," I say.

I tell them, I mostly love Socrates.
Especially because he continually picked
his ugly nose, a rare public pleasure

custodians miss in their daily work.
No one dares to think about it.

"Is it Kant's thoughts hanging over there?"
Foreigners ask me. He is from Kaliningrad.
"Holy moly. True it is."
"Strange frame, by the way."
What a wicked thing to say.

Lenin was in fact a busker.
Yet I have fallen truly in love
with a Soviet counter-revolution.
To all foreigners I must insist:
"the kisses are double up in here".

Ghosts. Writers. Underworld.

*There gathered in my mind the spirits of those
who are dead, writers, and unwedded philosophers,
and toil-worn red poets, and tender characters with hearts
yet old to fiction, and many, too, that were wounded
with space sickness, men slain in fights with themselves,
wearing their space costumes during a communist plague.*

Mayakovsky, I

He could drive the combine harvester
in the huge grain fields as if
it were a masculine revolution:
the assembly line of complex machinery
gathered the grain and shot it out
the side pipe, to unload
into waiting wagons.

In the shadow of his dark
mountain eyes, overlooking the
fertile fields from the wheelhouse,
a smoking cigarette glowed in the night
as a warning light ever calling.

The industrial hammer and sickle
seized the battlefields of nature:
ears of grain flaunted against the sky
soon to be cut down
by the cutter bar of steel.
"And what for?" Food for the people.
His starry fists stirred the soft soil.

The Vygotsky Buns

Outside the breakfast bakery in Aarhus C,
the children are waiting for the buns.
This is their zone of proximal development.
"Aren't the buns soon ready?" they ask,
their noses pressed against the pane.

Every sunny spring morning, Danish culture
settles in the children through the language
of class consciousness, in mighty, newly
constructed concrete apartment blocks,
near the roundabout of the military parade.

The ideologically bewitched bakery
has a rational and materialistic agenda:
the baker's freshly baked buns, with butter,
make small souls alive and happy.
These buns are the future of the people.

Cosmonaut 8000

the cosmonaut   goes   grassy
in his intergalactic bed   in outer space
his heart   is weightless   a vanishing
nothing   in the large   airless vacuum
and he   becomes   a modernist   avant-garde

8000-POET

The Red Space Cavalry

They nuked all the ladies
in the outer hemisphere.
Chopped down entire
civilizations of aliens
tough as Danish Vikings.

They gathered the reins
and tapped the pyramidal
monolith in front.
The atomic grenade
had burst the frontal lobes.

And then they stopped—
just outside the moon—
and pointed and said:
*"Comrades, Apollo 11
landed here in 1969.*

*Send by a hostile nation.
Let's shoot the moon
into gravel. Then no one
will remember the inferior
victory, ha ha ha."*

Horror Poem by Doctor Sputnik

Alas, I'm not the masculine hero
I would like to be. But then I see you,
Yelena. We are a story. At the log cabin
with the soft fire in the fireplace, we keep
operating on the dying patient in our souls.
Doors and windows are turned wide open,
birds are twittering and insects buzzing.

The poor woodcutters have found
the deep treasures in the nearby forest.

Long-Take Tarkovsky

I

It must be a fragile
and ramshackle house;
even the best bricks
crumble into dust.

Yet the house has a soul
in the gradual deconstruction
against the sky.

II

I can pull dreams
across the doorstep
of my house.

The fireplace is on fire
in the water-locked room.

I want to look
into the downfall?
But who will
hold me back?

III

I forget,
I am sitting on
rusted machinery
in these bleak
marshlands.

They carry me
completely
in all this mud.

I thank
the rain for it.

Yes, simply:
I am thanking
the rain.

Spacey Trascendence

In the back corner of my garden,
I saw Fyodor Dostoevsky
in the shadow of a lonely tree.

He had become a demon,
but as always, he was divided
between two worlds;
he never felt completely
at home in the beyond either.

Sitting in heaven, he had been
dreaming back to the this-worldly
and imagined he, step by step,
descended from the higher to the lower.

Thus in a short adverse revelation,
he materialized in my garden
to experience again how the unlimited
could be limited, the singular polyphonic
the infinite final and the perfect imperfect.

He sat looking around as a real shade,
noticed how time could fly again.
He lived a moment of relief
from the spiritual world;
felt the force of gravity
spinning in his legs - and
when a wind entered the garden,

he stayed sitting for a couple of seconds
before he again disappeared up
through the leaves of my lonely tree.

.

Soldier. Gamer. Loser.

There came up the spirit
of the great truth-teller from the underworld, and he spoke
in his polyphonic voice to me: Hero of Dissidence,
sprung from Thy, cosmonaut of Aarhus.
Why hast thou left the light of common sense?

Space Soldier

Because of some strange circumstances, I came into contact with the Space Army Center. I was living downtown Aarhus and had a regular job at a hot-dog stand to make some money, while I was developing my unique character as a space soldier. But one night during the winter, I had a total breakdown in one of the big tournaments. Even before the semi-finales, I bailed out and withdrew. The enemy couldn't be terminated in my usual straight clinical finish.

After the battle, I admitted to my team I totally lost track of the game. In the middle of an important battle, I started to think about my character. And I knew the player must be absolutely absorbed to maneuver efficiently. In front of the monitor, I reassured my friends it was a momentary relapse.

At first, my friends reacted a little irritated and put up a smiley and a thumbs up. They didn't pay any further attention to my suddenly occurred problem and kept on fighting one of the big battles. My girlfriend, Yelena, even sent me a love emoji and wrote that it was all right, I should be allowed to take a short break as a real cyberspace hero. She wrote I was a true space soldier and indispensable for the team. I hoped she was right.

*

Yet in the next battle, I continued my decline. After having lost track of the game again, I screamed, "I am out. I am out" And I was really out this time. I got knocked out in the first round —and I was scared; I didn't know what to do; my mind was in disarray. I started hearing a voice that said to me, "You are a regular copy"; on the other hand, I still strongly believed I was a real space soldier. It is all an evil dream, a hallucination that could maybe disappear again if I trained hard and thoroughly, I said to myself. And if I stayed in my delusion and worked it through, I could again dispense with this newly experienced deficiency. My character was playing me a kitty, I was pretty sure.

Gradually, it became worse and worse, my fighting abilities deteriorated completely. I couldn't stop my recently discovered weakness from taking hold. If I were a regular copy, I would not be able to be a unique soldier in the forthcoming great war between the new space armies. The consequences were devastating. My character would be looked upon as useless. I would become a bot and expelled from the great game because of my false appearance. I would have to leave my friends, since they could not take the chance of being teamed up or associated with me. My friends would all unfollow me; I was sure. Even my girlfriend would unfriend me.

*

One Monday afternoon, I couldn't keep it going any longer, when one of my customers at the hot-dog stand said I looked spacey behind the sliding safety partition, things went awry. Monday was early closing, and when I got home, I went straight to my bed and lay up there and could do nothing; I couldn't fight the brain-snipers in my mind alone. I surrendered and cried incessantly.

My friends from the team discovered from the video-camera that I was lying in my bed crying, and I told them I couldn't stand it. Of course, they noticed my gradual breakdown over the last few weeks, where I bailed-out countless times. I went on many solitary walks in the nearby battlefields. In the end, my girlfriend called the Space Army Center from her headset, and I got scheduled for an interview.

*

Yelena sent me an online invitation for her blue vehicle, her face reproduction looked surprised and worried at me in the message, and maybe she felt the same in real life, I don't know. We flew to the Space Army Center, and it all occurred to me like being thrown out of my life without a life-saving parachute. The Space Army Center was a looming neo-futuristic castle in a neon lighting on a little island in the sea outside our city. A majestic concrete building towered, unconquerable, against the sky in pure masculine granite.

I entered the office of a colonel in full armour. In front of her, I cried about my insolvable ambivalence, and told the colonel about my internal problems. The colonel told me I was ill, because I considered myself a regular copy. She asked

45

PETER GRAARUP WESTERGAARD

me if I played a soldier in the big games. I said I played soldier almost all the time. And she nodded, acknowledging.

I asked the colonel if those voices I heard about my regularity were true. Was my unconscious telling me I was a regular copy, something I should believe in? She explained to me I should probably admit I was a regular copy. These were messages from my unconscious. I became afraid: Was this true?

It was not the most well-chosen time to finally realize I was regular copy, my friends were gathering in troops. I probably ruined their war spirit. The soldier mustering was a true hell, even though my friends insisted they had a good night. I didn't believe them. They had a friend on the virtual battlefield who wasn't able to deliver in the fights. I sat quietly, trying to hide my problems.

My troop took part in a minor insurgency, and it was successful, against all odds. In the United States, I was told, some news-websites published articles on my troop maneuvering brilliantly, especially in the counterstrike, but I was not happy with the compliment.

I was embarrassed, felt I played a false hero all my life, because I now felt total defeat: the feeling of not being myself in the literal sense and the same time, doomed to remain a regular copy. Everything went smoothly on the surface, but the depth of it was all a jumble, a chaos I tried to hide during the battle.

The irony was, of course, I was beginning my time as a unique virtual sniper, which I signed up for a few months before my strange new inclinations. Before I collapsed. My studies in virtual physical fighting were side-tracked, so I decided I'd rather become a virtual sniper—I could do something generally appreciated and maybe heal from my dawning weakness. Yet it didn't help me at all, my skills were inevitably deteriorating. I was leaving the game as a bot.

*

My girlfriend did not know what to do to help me, but she contacted her supervisor, who was a knowledgeable intelligence officer, and recommended the special general AI whom I should visit at the Space Army Center. It was not easy to consult the special general AI because I was behind on vital points. Once again, I felt like being thrown out of my safe game without a parachute.

I didn't gain much profit from talking to others, for I was constantly paranoid they now believed me to be a regular copy. I had a hard time holding on to my true self. My ability to understand, as well as my general awareness in the fighting, was diminished as my thoughts circulated in swirls inside my head.

The next day I flew to the high castle; this time guided to the turrets. The whiteness and sterility of the atmosphere devastated me, and my mood was not improved by my first encounter with the special general AI who was supposed to help. The general AI hovered in space while it talked. It was strange, like a conversation in an old computer game with no emotions involved: pure objective exchange of stark signs in space without any gravity.

The general AI asked me several things, whether I had regular thoughts. I said "yes," but at the same time, I assured the AI, I created them myself or they might come from my headset. But the general AI was not interested, or it did not hear it because of technical disabilities, the general AI asked me to repeat things several times. I spoke loudly, yet it could barely register through the large hearing device. The AI contraption seemed without commitment to my problem, which I also exaggerated greatly when I had it damn terrible—bordering on the unbearable, whatever it might mean. Was I a regular copy? It all hovered in space.

The general AI was programmed with an objective checklist. Finally, it gave me the verdict: I was, in fact, a space soldier (but with a second identity). I didn't have to worry anymore. The AI said I was becoming a gifted soldier and I could possibly get over my regularity. At the same time, I was given the opportunity to get into the special space troops who were going to fight Team Soviet Army when they first arrived in the space in front of us. But medicine would improve my fighting abilities.

*

My girlfriend, Yelena, followed me every step online when I went for the drug. She guided me to the door when I walked to the pharmacy for the pills. She could see me walking with heavy steps, when I left her behind and crossed the street, she told me afterwards. I turned off my interface.

When I got online again, I took the medicine; and she put the controller to her face. She shed a few tears and said, "What's going on? My love? My dearest @Sputnik Peter!" She waved affectionately. "What's wrong with you? Can't you forget it—can't you do something about it yourself?" She asked me from the monitor.

I apologized greatly; I was so sorry, not only because I was so awful but because my girlfriend was so upset and because she was having soldier's mustering the next day. The soldiers would log in; there was going to be a battle in space all night. My girlfriend pulled herself together, started the spacecraft, and flew home to her starting point. She was accustomed to pulling herself together all her life, for she suffered from bullying in school when she was a teenager. Yet she worked hard every day in school, toiling and improving with her strong will.

"Where there's a will, there's a way," She always said to me when we were losing a game. She asked gently on the monitor if I could find this will. But I couldn't, even though I so endlessly wanted to. My mind was working against itself. Gradually, I was becoming a regular copy, I felt.

*

The medication was terrible in the beginning, but after some time, I started to feel stronger, even invincible. I looked at the heavy-armed steel closet in the living room. Before, I couldn't possibly lift that closet myself, but suddenly, I lifted the entire closet with one hand. It was amazing. I called my Yelena on my monitor, I wanted to show her something important. I was ready for the war. I could lift the closet with the tip of my fingers. Without the controller as the intermediary, I was the chosen one.

Sickness. Future. Jesus.

Yet hear me: when my wars are over,
I will land on Thy's sandy shore.
There I shall live and be honoured
and no longer be self-divided and online.
Yet more—in my true reality, Jesus
will be my guide with his true socialism.

Spacey Peter's Epiphany

I agree that ghosts only appear to the sick,
but that only proves that they are unable to appear
except to the sick, not that they don't exist.
—Fyodor Dostoyevsky

a.

The divine buzz from heaven,
blowing from behind the doors,
through cracks and under windowsills.

God always finds a rupture in my house.
The angels sing sharply and howling.
I hold my ears.
The heavenly song,
a penetrating storm,
a trembling vibration in my weak flesh.

b.

In the mirror I see myself:
I am deformed.
With long legs and a bloated body—
I am swelling with an imaginary moon sickness.

Angels sing
heavenly spheres.
I'll see and hear things,

others cannot see and hear,
a strange curse.

c.

The sun is licking me.
And I've got an eye on the forehead.

Satan seeks me.
His voice is a whip,
I'm receptive flesh.

d.

Around me are dead flowers.
A strange fire
has incinerated everything.

Satan's drought crackles like a mighty bonfire.
"I'm going to be the new gardener,"
I say to myself.
Jesus will be the water.
God the very life,
I can dream into existence.

To My Tsarina

If you are standing in front of the abyss of death, run away.
Run as fast as you can. Run into the safe land.
And hide behind the mountains, in the woods, or in the dense grass.

You have always been a tsarina,
even now, when you must hide
from the spreading death,
like a simple farm girl.

But wherever you are in the mountains, I will come
and guide you across the dangerous gap,
every time you get out of the woods,
I will lead you to a better hiding place.

I will keep the fields safe,
until the day when you wish
to lie free in the green grass.

See, my *tsaritsa*: death cannot find you now. The abyss is too far away.
As long as you hide yourself from death,
you can live. As long as you hide yourself from death,
I can live.

I will never tell you this: I survive because of you.

I will encircle you with my words.
When I call you an everlasting rose,
death will wonder at
this infinitely beautiful flower that can never fade.
And he will have to walk away from the garden,
in which you forever flourish.

I will be on duty night and day,
a few meters from you.
Death will never ever be allowed to pick your life.
Break your stalk.
Begin your death.

True Socialism

Jesus was an odd man. He always
understood everything. Already
as a little boy, he could understand
more than the learned scribes
could know.

Mostly he walked around
by himself. He spoke to God
or to what was divine in his soul.
In a way, his thoughts were not
big or profound. His ideas were not
particularly complicated. But
unhappy people became happy.

His disciples could see something
in him. They recognized themselves
when people anointed his feet
and felt liberated from their
inner sufferings—if only he had
said to them, "Go away."

Dissent. Critique. Voyage.

I am a young man of dissidence and lovesickness,
who was caught in outer space after I sacked
the pandemic mind-space of Aarhus. Many were the men
affected by my dissident thoughts, aye, and many
the woes I suffered in outer space, seeking to win
my life back and the return of my Soviet comrades.

Dissidence

I've become a dirty white
angel, a single snowflake
in the wind of the cold
contaminated universe,
who whispers truths into
the ear canals of people.

Listen

A Political Education

We are always an intermediary
in the fast openings. Our jelly backbone
ends a long, slow journey.
Almost cooked? Yes. The world
of the fast days turns like a neglected
globe in overcrowded children's rooms
where plastic-polluted seas shine
like shoals of illuminating pearls.

The sun is at the center,
a socialist mom finally realizes:
educating the earth's population
is completely impossible.

The Prison Satellite

1

// in outer space / the prison satellite hovers / with communication criminals / among them am I / the poor pope Sputnik / in the cells of the rotating space-prison / the one-eyed system / XCE10000 in the middle informs / about perfect communication / in small parables / we listen / to a synthetic meat mouth / with a juicy, voluminous voice / it explains the philosophy of the one-eyed system XCE10000 / there is an important message / in everything / the mouth says / everything is conscious / nothing is subconscious / all good communicative morals / says the meat mouth / while licking its lips / if a conversation partner addresses you /and you want to make it clear to him / you have understood him / you say / now I know what I have to relate to / thus you have signaled / you understand him / your mental state / has reached stability / from which it does not matter / whether the interlocutor repeats his sentence or not //

2

//understanding is immunizing yourself against the stimulus / constituted by the perception of the message / it is to choose the right behaviour in relation to the situation / you are in / all words, all sentences / all linguistic expressions tell / about the great moral-improvement story / the inmates are reprogrammed / by the one-eyed XCE10000 system / many of you inmates have been unjustifiably / promoted by the establishment / Facebook and Instagram / the state was totally incapable of catching you / the government believed in you and your stories / given you rank and prestige / without deserving it in any way / you have good cheating and deception skills / you are intelligent but morally depraved / and that's it," says / the leading judge, Ulysses Lex Slatem / (former system critic) / in the main office of the prison satellite / in a very concise manner //

3

// the prison satellite is a place of transformation / the meat mouth spits out a word trap / that works itself into the brain of the prisoners / as chemotherapy against communication cancer

/ in the misdeveloped brains / the meat mouth of the polyprison satellite / sucks all metastases out / with its mouth / it chops up misused words and phrases / as language puke / sends the waste out into the endless toilet of the universe //

4

// it's the one-eyed system XCE10000 / who decides / what is true or false perception / the system determines / what all words unmistakably mean /—within a certain framework—/ but the system does not have to be visible or present / to determine what all words mean / the prisoners in the prison satellite / are remodelled in the one-eyed XCE10000 character system / we float weightless in the cells / isolated from all communicative noise / slowly we become / properly communicating / individuals //

The Great Escape

I will tell about a man whose fate and exploits
should rightly be found among the writings of all peoples.

- Ludvig Holberg

I left the prison satellite XCE10000,

                            I was TOO INNOCENT.

"Listen popeyed Peter, I'd like you to go Phoenix XZ instead

and say these things, forget about Yelena, forget about Yelena,

for it can't be true

                         you tell stories like this here,

Sputnik Peter," says Calypso.

I am sitting in the spacecraft DOGG/2,

                            and it can't be decided

if I'm really psychotic or a covidiot

                    by the supreme health authorities.

I dream a dream,

repeatedly,

where

I

walk

down

a

staircase

a MORE THAN a

hundred

meters'

long

decrease.

And at the bottom of the underworld of books

I find a rebuilt hell: Yelena is gone.

O horror, oh!

I am again the guffy-minded duffer,

who can't clap the cone—

who is a complete ball-oaf and a sports-lubber.

CALLED-OUT by noon.

2

Nor did I pay my bills, Calypso

my indulgences,

              my sin, I didn't keep a distance

and I'm afraid

            to be accused of being a scammer.

exposed to public derision,

                in the tabloid gossip columns,

on SOCIAL MEDIA

                      or on the

square
in front of the church—

on display in the middle of Store Torv—

                or in front of Aarhus town hall itself.

And yet I trespass everything to the boundaries.

                      Use rules,

God,
and

the dialectics of Marx,

Soviet law and the traffic law of the universe,
and I bend them as I please.

Hi, hi

        I'm a rebuilt

Red Ford Mustang Coupe Car

           from the machine halls

on the outskirts of the Danish Northwest.

3

And SEXY Calypso doesn't even bother.

> She won't have sex with

me—at all

> —Isn't that what she

came for?

She didn't even bother to look at my thick belly.

> As big as a pricey rebuilt
> Red Ford Mustang Coupe Car.

"I sometimes get a cerebral meltdown.
I have to get it all out, absolutely—and
many different kinds of people
suddenly have to listen to my agony," I say to Calypso.

She thinks I'm going to visit Phoenix XZ from the inner circles. "You go, girlboy".

But Phoenix XZ doesn't care.

> He will give a fuck.

> Because there is so much to do—

Especially, the shit,

all that fucking shit,

the psychopharmacies, pharmaceuticals,
YOU HAVE BEEN ON. EVERYONE HAS

BEEN ON. Inside, which should be the outside

I say so much—all the time:

Sputnik Peter, who am I really? From this isolated perspective of the universe?

I don't know.

Of course, I do know

I come straight from a machine hall on the outskirts,

but metaphysically speaking, I do not know

at all,

where I come from   or where I am going

or who the fuck I am,

do I?

Space. Disappearance. Zero.

Thus my comrades gathered on Store Torv and observed the sky:
they extinguished the grief with pilsners, defied the restrictions
and tried to forget the nasty fire the poetry spread.
With grieving minds, friends and comrades finally unleashed
the traveling satellite while tears were running down their cheeks.
They laid the poems down in a golden shrine;
around them, they wrapped the finest red robes of hammer and sickle.
When the morning came,
they went to Aarhus Space Station.

Acknowledgement

Dear reader, please bear in mind that this is a work of fiction and imagination. Space and time have been rearranged to suit the convenience of the book, and with the exception of public figures and writers, any resemblance to persons living or dead is coincidental. Furthermore, the role played by different public figures, cities, organizations and writers in this collection is also entirely fictional. The opinions expressed are those of the fictional characters and the protagonist Spacey Peter and should not be confused with the author's.

"Mayakovsky, I" has been longlisted in The Fish Publishing Poetry Prize 2020 by Billy Collins.

"The Trojan Love Machine" has been published in MuseIndia in the June 2021 issue.

"The Museum of Ideas" has first been published in another version in The Bangalore Review in the May 2020 issue.

The Homeric interludes, as well as the prologue and epilogue, are all inspired by and borrowed from Alexander Pope's translation of the Iliad and the Odyssey into the English language.

The introductory quote to the whole collection is borrowed from Walter Benjamin, Moscow Diary (Translated by Richard Sieburth).

The interlude to "The Museum of Ideas" is from the essay The Proper Study of Mankind: An Anthology of Essays (1997) by Isaiah Berlin.

PETER GRAARUP WESTERGAARD

The interlude to "Spacy Peter's Epiphany" is from the novel Crime and Punishment by Fyodor Dostoevsky (Translated by Constance Garbett).

The interlude to "The Great Escape" is from Ludvig Holberg, Peder Paars (Translated by Peter Graarup Westergaard).

The prose poem "Yet No Contamination" is inspired by Thucydides, History of the Peloponnesian War.

The list of pandemic diseases in the poem "The Health-Care System" is based on the WHO-website: https://www.who.int/emergencies/diseases/en/ Accessed 01.02.2021.

The poem "Space Jealousy" is inspired by Sappho's poem "Sappho 31."

Part of the thinking in "Dissidence III" is based on the semiotics of René Frédéric Thom.

About the Author

Peter Graarup Westergaard

Peter Graarup Westergaard has published the poetry collection Nordvest (2017), also translated into English and Danish Northwest (2019). He completed his MA in Comparative Literature at Aarhus University (2004) and holds a degree in English Literature also from Aarhus University (2015). He has also studied English Literature at Concordia University Montreal (2000-2001) and philosophy at Oxford University, Department of Continuing Education (2018-2020). He teaches Danish, English and philosophy at a secondary boarding school in Denmark.

Lightning Source UK Ltd.
Milton Keynes UK
UKHW012241081022
410109UK00007B/868